The Radical Art of Self-Love

Embrace Your Authentic Self with Self-Love

Deepak Singh

pencil

ISBN 978-93-5667-714-2

Published in India 2023 by Pencil

A brand of
One Point Six Technologies Pvt. Ltd.
Unit no. 26, Ground Floor, Building A1,
Wadala Truck Terminal Road,
Near Post Office, Antop Hill, Mumbai - 400037
E connect@thepencilapp.com
W www.thepencilapp.com

DISCLAIMER: *The opinions expressed in this book are those of the authors and do not purport to reflect the views of the Publisher.*

Author biography

Hello! Happy to meet you, I'm Deepak Singh. I work as a research analyst and am passionate about writing books and doing research on the planet Earth, space, and the art of living. I most likely have high analytical and critical thinking abilities that enable me to assess data, spot trends, and reach conclusions in my capacity as a research analyst. As part of my job, I might perform primary and secondary research, analyze available data, and provide findings to guide individual, corporate, or organizational decision-making. I adore writing and researching as interests in space and Earth in my free time. You can tell that I have an open mind and am interested in learning about the world around me.

CONTENTS

Introduction

For good reason, the concept of self-love has received a lot of attention in recent years. Our self-esteem influences every part of our life, from our relationships to our work choices. However, self-love is more than just taking bubble baths and repeating happy affirmations. It is a daring act that necessitates bravery, openness, and a willingness to face our deepest fears and insecurities. We will look at the radical art of self-love and present practical ways for creating a more loving and compassionate connection with oneself in this book.

In a world that frequently prioritizes work over self-care, the concept of self-love has gained popularity in recent years. However, self-love is more than just taking bubble baths and repeating happy affirmations. It is a daring act that necessitates bravery, openness, and a willingness to face our deepest fears and insecurities.

The truth is that many of us struggle with genuinely loving ourselves. We may be carrying emotional scars from our history, or we may have internalized cultural messages telling us we are insufficient. We may engage in self-defeating behaviors such as self-criticism and self-doubt, or we may fail to set boundaries in our relationships.

However, the advantages of self-love go far beyond ourselves. We become better spouses, friends, and colleagues when we prioritize our own well-being. We have increased our productivity, resilience, and compassion for others.

We will look at the radical art of self-love and present practical ways for creating a more loving and compassionate connection with oneself in this book. We'll look at what self-love is and isn't, as well as the roles of self-acceptance, vulnerability, and sincerity in fostering self-love.

We will also examine how self-love can be a powerful tool for healing emotional scars from our past, establishing boundaries in our relationships, and overcoming self-doubt and self-criticism. Finally, we will discuss how to make self-love a daily practice through journaling, mindfulness, and affirmations.

We may establish a more positive relationship with ourselves and improve all aspects of our life by prioritizing self-love. This book is for everyone who wants to nurture more self-love and is willing to accept the radical act of putting their own well-being first.

Chapter 1 Self-Love Definition

In this chapter, we'll look at what self-love is and isn't. We will examine the distinction between self-love and self-care and discuss why self-love is so important to our general well-being.

Self-love is a concept that has gained popularity in recent years, but what precisely does it imply? Self-love is a complex and nuanced concept that requires a thorough awareness of one's own needs, goals, and beliefs.

Self-love is defined as sincere respect and acceptance of oneself. This incorporates both positive and negative elements of oneself. Self-love does not imply being perfect or always feeling good about oneself, but rather recognizing and accepting all aspects of oneself, even the tough or uncomfortable ones.

Setting appropriate boundaries and taking care of oneself physically, emotionally, and psychologically are also aspects of self-love. Self-care activities include exercise, a healthy diet, meditation, therapy, and spending time with loved ones.

Cultivating a pleasant and loving inner dialogue is another part of self-love. This entails treating oneself with compassion and understanding rather than harsh self-criticism. It also entails identifying and confronting harmful thought patterns, as well as replacing them with more positive and powerful ones.

Self-love is not selfish; rather, it is a necessary component of general happiness. It is easier to love people and build healthy relationships when one loves oneself. Furthermore, self-love can assist individuals in making better decisions, setting objectives, and pursuing their passions and interests.

Self-love is ultimately a journey and a lifetime practice. It necessitates a dedication to oneself as well as a determination to always learn and progress. It may entail questioning society's standards or ideas that encourage negative self-talk or self-destructive behavior. It may also be necessary to seek assistance from trusted friends, family, or experts.

To summarise, defining self-love is a complex and multifaceted process, but it eventually boils down to totally accepting and respecting oneself. Setting appropriate boundaries, practicing self-care, establishing a good inner dialogue, and recognizing the value of one's own well-being are all part of it. Individuals can enjoy happier, healthier, and more fulfilled lives by practicing self-love.

Chapter 2 Understanding the Value of Self-Love

Many of us find it difficult to prioritize self-love because we perceive it as selfish or self-indulgent. However, the advantages of self-love go far beyond ourselves. In this chapter, we will look at how self-love can improve our relationships, productivity, and general quality of life.

A healthy and fulfilling existence is built on self-love. It is the act of loving and caring for oneself, both physically and psychologically. Self-love is an essential component of personal growth and development, and it has several advantages that help all aspects of our lives. We will look at the benefits of self-love and how it can improve our mental and physical health, relationships, and overall well-being in this chapter.

- **Improved Mental Health:**Improved mental health is one of the most significant advantages of self-love. We learn to accept and love ourselves unconditionally when we practice self-love. We become more conscious of our thoughts and emotions, and we learn to control them in a healthy way. This results in increased emotional stability and resilience, which can help us cope with stress, anxiety, and depression. Furthermore, self-love aids in the development of a positive self-image. We learn to value our strengths and accept our flaws. This results in enhanced self-confidence and self-esteem, which can improve our relationships and overall quality of life.

- **Better Physical Health:**There are various physical health benefits to self-love. When we practice self-love, we prioritize our physical health by eating healthily, getting adequate sleep, and engaging in regular physical activity. This results in improved overall health and a lower chance of chronic diseases. Furthermore, when we love ourselves, we are more inclined to engage in self-care practices that enhance physical health, such as regular check-ups at the doctor and seek medical help when necessary. We also tend to indulge in fewer unhealthy behaviors, such as excessive smoking and drinking.

- **Improved Relationships:**Self-love can also strengthen our interpersonal interactions. We are better equipped to love and accept others when we love and accept ourselves. We are more compassionate, sensitive, and forgiving, which can lead to more satisfying relationships. Furthermore, when we love ourselves, we are less likely to engage in codependent behaviors that can be destructive to our relationships. We are better able to establish appropriate boundaries, convey our needs, and maintain our independence, which can improve our relationships and general well-being.

- **Increased Productivity and Success:**Self-esteem can boost our productivity and achievement. We have a higher sense of self-awareness and clarity about our aims and values when we practice self-love. This enables us to make better judgments and take activities that are more in line with our genuine selves, leading to more success and fulfillment in our personal and professional lives. Furthermore, self-love aids in the removal of self-doubt and the dread of failure. We build a growth attitude and become more resilient in the face of adversity. This results in greater productivity, creativity, and invention, all of which can benefit our professional success.

In conclusion, Self-love is a powerful force that may improve many aspects of our existence. We may improve our mental and physical health, relationships, and overall well-being by practicing self-love. We learn to unconditionally love and accept ourselves, which permits us to love and accept others more profoundly. Self-love is a lifelong adventure that takes time and practice, but the rewards are well worth the effort.

Chapter 3 Self-Acceptance's Role in Self-Love

Self-acceptance is required for self-love. In this chapter, we'll look at why accepting ourselves as we are is such an important part of developing self-love. We'll also talk about how to practice self-acceptance even when it's difficult.

Self-acceptance and self-love are frequently linked since both are necessary for creating a positive self-image and a healthy connection with oneself. The practice of recognizing and accepting one's own strengths, shortcomings, and unique qualities without judgment or criticism is referred to as self-acceptance. In contrast, self-love refers to the practice of caring for oneself, prioritizing one's needs, and treating oneself with respect and compassion. In this chapter, we'll look at the function of self-acceptance in fostering self-love and the advantages of doing so.

Acceptance of oneself is the first step towards self-love. It is hard to love oneself completely unless one accepts oneself. Because of cultural expectations, past traumas, and negative self-talk, many people struggle with self-acceptance. Self-acceptance entails identifying one's imperfections and accepting them as a part of oneself, rather than attempting to conceal or correct them. It also entails recognizing and appreciating one's own abilities rather than downplaying or ignoring them.

Increased self-esteem is one of the most important advantages of self-acceptance. We are less prone to compare ourselves to others and engage in negative self-talk when we accept ourselves for who we are. Instead, we should concentrate on our accomplishments and qualities, which can lead to a more positive self-image and a stronger sense of self-worth. This, in turn, can lead to more confidence and a greater willingness to take chances and achieve our objectives.

Self-acceptance is also important for mental health. We are more prone to experience unpleasant emotions such as shame, guilt, and worry when we reject or criticize ourselves. These feelings can be harmful to our mental health and well-being. Self-acceptance, on the other hand, can lead to increased emotional stability and resilience. It can also assist us in developing a more optimistic attitude in life, leading to more pleasure and fulfillment.

Self-acceptance can also strengthen our interpersonal interactions. We are less prone to seek affirmation or acceptance from others when we accept ourselves. This allows us to be ourselves and express our actual feelings and wants, which can lead to more authentic and rewarding relationships. Furthermore, self-acceptance can lead to more empathy and compassion for others since we are better able to recognize and embrace their distinct features and viewpoints.

Finally, self-acceptance is an essential component of self-love. We can build a more positive self-image, increased self-esteem, and greater emotional stability by accepting ourselves for who we are. It can also strengthen our interpersonal relationships and lead to more happiness and fulfillment. While accepting ourselves can be difficult, it is a worthy practice that can have a big impact on our general well-being.

Chapter 4 Wound Healing Through Self-Love

Many of us carry emotional scars from our past that limit our ability to truly love and accept ourselves. We will look at how self-love may be a strong tool for healing these traumas and developing a more positive self-image in this chapter.

Self-love is defined as the act of loving, embracing, and caring for oneself. Self-love is critical for our entire health, particularly when it comes to mending emotional traumas. We may experience pain, anger, or despair when we have emotional wounds. We may, however, heal these scars by loving ourselves.

Recognizing Emotional Wounds

Negative experiences or traumas, such as childhood maltreatment, a failed relationship, or a tragic occurrence, generate emotional wounds. These encounters might leave us hurt, angry, or anxious. Emotional scars can also lead to self-defeating ideas, such as feeling unworthy or unlovable.

The Importance of Self-Love in Healing

In numerous ways, self-love can aid in the healing of emotional traumas. For starters, it assists us in accepting ourselves and our experiences. Instead of denying or repressing our sentiments, self-love encourages us to acknowledge and validate them. Second, self-love assists us in forgiving ourselves and others. Forgiveness is an important part of the healing process, and self-love makes it easier to let go of previous hurts and move on. Finally, self-love assists us in developing positive views about ourselves, such as feeling worthy of love and respect.

Steps for Practising Self-Love, Here are some measures you can take to practice self-love and heal emotional wounds:

- **Practise Self-Care:**Self-care is a necessary component of self-love. Taking care of yourself physically, psychologically, and emotionally contributes to increased self-esteem and confidence. Eat healthily, exercise regularly, get enough sleep, and engage in things that offer you joy and relaxation.

- **Establish Boundaries:**Setting boundaries is an important aspect of self-love. It assists you in prioritizing your requirements and shielding yourself from harmful influences. To preserve healthy relationships and avoid burnout, practice creating healthy boundaries in your relationships and at work.

- **Practice Positive Self-Talk:**Good self-talk is a strong skill that can assist you in developing good beliefs about yourself. Replace negative self-talk with affirmations like "I am worthy of love and respect" or "I am capable and deserving of success."

- **Seek Help:**Healing emotional scars can be difficult, and it's good to seek help from others. Discuss your feelings and experiences with a trusted friend, family member, or therapist. Seeking help can help you obtain a new perspective and make you feel less alone.

Finally, emotional traumas can be healed via self-love. You can create a strong sense of self-love and heal your emotional traumas by practicing self-care, creating healthy boundaries, using positive self-talk, and seeking support. Remember that self-love is a lifelong process, not a one-time event. Be gentle with yourself and practice self-love on a daily basis.

Chapter 5 Boundaries and Self-Love

Boundaries are an important part of self-love. In this chapter, we'll look at how creating boundaries in our relationships can help us create a more loving relationship with ourselves.

Boundaries and self-love are two interconnected concepts that are critical for maintaining good relationships with oneself and others. A deep admiration and acceptance of oneself, including one's qualities, shortcomings, and limits, is referred to as self-love. Boundaries, on the other hand, are the boundaries we impose on our interactions with others in order to maintain our sense of self and protect ourselves from harm. This chapter will look at the significance of self-love and boundaries, how they are related, and how to cultivate both in our life.

The Value of Self-Love

Self-love is essential because it allows us to form a positive relationship with ourselves. We are more likely to take care of our physical, emotional, and mental well-being when we love ourselves. We are also more likely to pursue our goals and desires, and less likely to accept less in life than we deserve. Self-love can also help us build resilience and cope with adversity by allowing us to recognize our own worth and value even in adverse circumstances.

Self-esteem can also improve our interpersonal interactions. We are more likely to treat others with respect and kindness when we love ourselves since we see that others are also deserving of love and respect. Self-love can also help us set appropriate boundaries in our relationships since we are less inclined to accept damaging or disrespectful behavior.

The Value of Boundaries

Boundaries are crucial because they help us identify ourselves and our values. They enable us to safeguard our bodily, emotional, and mental well-being and keep us from being exploited or mistreated by others. Boundaries also assist us in communicating our needs and expectations to others, which can help to avoid misunderstandings and conflict.

Healthy limits are adaptable and can be modified as needed based on the circumstances. They should be founded on our own values, beliefs, and wants, not on what others demand of us. Instead of feeling pressured to continually please others, healthy boundaries include expressing "no" when necessary and "yes" when we want to.

The Relationship Between Self-Love and Boundaries

Self-love and boundaries are inextricably linked because good boundaries necessitate a strong feeling of self-worth and self-respect. When we love ourselves, we are more inclined to establish boundaries that preserve our well-being and keep us from being abused or exploited. Setting and maintaining healthy boundaries, on the other hand, might help us develop self-love by reinforcing our feeling of self-worth and self-respect.

Developing Self-Love and Boundaries

Self-love and limits are lifelong processes that involve self-reflection, practice, and patience. Here are some suggestions for developing self-love and boundaries:

- **Practice self-care:**Self-care entails taking care of one's physical, emotional, and mental well-being through activities that nourish one, such as exercise, meditation, or spending time with loved ones.

- **Set aside time for introspection:**Consider your values, beliefs, and wants, and how these impact your interactions with others.

- **Practice saying "no" when necessary:**Saying "no" when necessary can be challenging, but it is crucial for setting healthy boundaries and maintaining your well-being.

- **Surround yourself with positive influences:**Spend time with individuals who encourage and uplift you rather than those who drain your vitality.

- **Seek help when needed:**If you are having difficulty with self-love or setting boundaries, seek help from a therapist or other mental health expert.

Finally, self-love and limits are two interwoven concepts that are critical for our general health and healthy relationships. Boundaries help us define and protect ourselves, while self-love allows us to respect and embrace ourselves. Developing self-love and boundaries involves deliberate and continuous work, which includes self-reflection, making time for self-care, and getting help when necessary. We can live a more happy and honest life and form deeper and more meaningful connections with others by building self-love and limits.

Chapter 6 Overcoming Self-Criticism and Doubt

Self-doubt and self-criticism can be big impediments to developing self-love. In this chapter, we will look at why we participate in these self-destructive behaviors and offer techniques for overcoming them.

Self-doubt and self-criticism are frequent emotions that many people encounter at some point in their life. Personal insecurities, societal pressures, or past experiences can all contribute to these feelings. While these feelings can be overwhelming, there are strategies to overcome them and boost one's self-esteem. This chapter will look at several methods for dealing with self-doubt and self-criticism.

- **Recognize the Source of Your Doubts and Criticism:**Identifying the origins of self-doubt and self-criticism is the first step towards conquering them. Many factors can contribute to self-doubt and self-criticism, including prior failures, negative self-talk, comparisons to others, and cultural pressures. Individuals can better comprehend and resolve these emotions by identifying the source of them.

- **Combat Negative Self-Talk:**Self-doubt and self-criticism are frequently caused by negative self-talk. Breaking the habit of negative self-talk might be difficult, but it is a necessary step in developing self-confidence. Recognizing negative self-talk and reframing it in a positive perspective is one method for combating it. For example, if a person thinks, "I'll never be able to do this," they can reframe the concept to, "I may struggle at first, but with practice, I can improve."

- **Concentrate on your strengths:**Focusing on strengths rather than faults is another method to overcome self-doubt and self-criticism. Individuals can make a list of their successes and strengths to refer to when they feel self-doubt creeping in. This list can include both personal and professional accomplishments, no matter how minor they are. Individuals can gain self-confidence and recognize their potential by focusing on their strengths.

- **Set attainable goals:**Setting attainable goals can also help people overcome self-doubt and self-criticism. When unrealistic expectations are not met, they can be overpowering and lead to self-doubt. Individuals can gain confidence when they achieve reasonable goals, leading to more success in the future.

- **Positive People Should Surround You:**Being with positive individuals can also help one overcome self-doubt and self-criticism. Unpleased people can depress others and reinforce unpleasant thoughts and sentiments. Positive people, on the other side, can offer support, encouragement, and motivation.

- **Self-care is essential:**Finally, practicing self-care can assist people in overcoming self-doubt and self-criticism. Exercise, meditation, spending time with loved ones, and following a hobby are all examples of self-care activities. Self-care can improve mood and confidence, resulting in greater resilience in the face of self-doubt and self-criticism.

In Conclusion, while self-doubt and self-criticism are frequent experiences, they do not have to define a person. Individuals can overcome self-doubt and self-criticism and improve self-confidence by recognizing its cause, confronting negative self-talk, concentrating on strengths, creating realistic objectives, surrounding themselves with supportive people, and practicing self-care. Individuals can go on with greater resilience and attain their goals if they keep these strategies in mind.

Chapter 7 Embracing Vulnerability and Authenticity

Self-love necessitates openness and truthfulness. This chapter will look at why it might be difficult to be real in our relationships and offer suggestions for accepting vulnerability as a way to greater self-love.

There has been a growing awareness and appreciation for the value of vulnerability and authenticity in our personal and professional lives in recent years. Accepting vulnerability entails being open to sharing our actual thoughts, feelings, and experiences with others, even if it makes us feel vulnerable or uncertain. Authenticity, on the other hand, refers to being true to oneself, one's ideals, and one's views. In this chapter, we will look at the advantages of accepting vulnerability and authenticity, as well as how we might develop these qualities in ourselves.

The Advantages of Adopting Vulnerability and Authenticity:

- **Relationships Improved:** When we are willing to be vulnerable with others, we open the door to deeper and more meaningful connections. Vulnerability enables us to be open and honest about our feelings and experiences, which builds trust and empathy.

- **Increased Resilience:**Accepting vulnerability involves admitting that we are not flawless and that we may make mistakes or face difficulties. This thinking enables us to develop resilience and recover more rapidly from setbacks.

- **Greater Self-Awareness:**Being authentic implies being true to oneself, which necessitates a high level of self-awareness. We grow more in tune with our own thoughts and feelings when we embrace our vulnerabilities and reveal our actual selves to others.

- **Enhanced Creativity:**Being vulnerable and real can also lead to increased creativity and innovation. We are more likely to come up with new and creative ideas when we are willing to take chances and be genuine with ourselves.

Developing Vulnerability and Authenticity

- **Practise Self-Acceptance:**Accepting ourselves for who we are, flaws and all, is a prerequisite for embracing vulnerability and authenticity. Practice self-compassion and remind yourself that being imperfect is okay.

- **Build Trusting Relationships:**Surround yourself with individuals you can trust and with whom you can be vulnerable. This could be friends, relatives, or coworkers.

- **Begin modestly:**Accepting vulnerability might be intimidating, so begin with modest steps. Share a personal experience with a trusted friend, or speak up in a professional meeting.

- **Active Listening:**When we are vulnerable with others, we must also actively listen to their experiences and emotions. This results in a mutually beneficial and helpful partnership.

- **Consider Your Values:**Being honest necessitates an understanding of your values and ideas. Take some time to consider what is important to you and how you may live in accordance with those ideals.

Finally, while embracing vulnerability and authenticity might be difficult, the rewards are well worth the effort. We may improve our relationships, raise our resilience, create greater self-awareness, and boost our creativity by fostering these qualities in ourselves. Remember that vulnerability and authenticity are not flaws, but rather assets that can assist us in living more fulfilled and meaningful lives.

Chapter 8 Making Self-Compassion a Daily Practice

Self-love is a daily practice, not a one-time event. In this chapter, we will discuss how to make self-love a habit through journaling, mindfulness, and affirmations.

Self-love is a crucial component of our happiness and mental wellness. It aids in the development of a strong feeling of self-worth, self-acceptance, and self-confidence. Making self-love a regular practice can have a significant impact on many aspects of our lives, from our relationships to our careers and personal growth. In this chapter, we will look at how we might nurture self-love on a daily basis.

Develop Self-Awareness: Self-awareness is the first step towards making self-love a daily practice. We can understand our ideas, emotions, and behaviors when we are self-aware. We can discover places in our lives where we need to practice self-love by becoming conscious of our patterns and behaviors. We can then make a conscious effort to adjust our beliefs and behaviors in order to achieve our self-love objectives.

- **Exercise Gratitude:**Gratitude is an effective method for developing self-love. It allows us to focus on the good things in our lives and appreciate what we have. We can redirect our emphasis from what we lack to what we have by taking a few minutes each day to write down things we are grateful for. This alteration in viewpoint has the potential to significantly affect our self-esteem and overall well-being.

- **Exercise Self-Compassion:**The practice of treating oneself with love, understanding, and acceptance is known as self-compassion. It entails admitting our flaws and failings without passing judgment or condemnation. We can improve our self-esteem and establish a more positive self-image by practicing self-compassion.

- **Self-care is essential:**Self-care is a necessary component of self-love. It entails looking after our physical, emotional, and mental wellness. Exercise, meditation, journaling, and spending time with loved ones are examples of self-care activities. We may improve our general well-being and establish a more positive self-image by prioritizing self-care.

- **Establish Limits:**Setting limits is an important part of self-love. It entails saying no to things that do not serve us and establishing boundaries for what we are ready to endure. Setting limits allows us to protect our time, energy, and resources while avoiding burnout and stress.

- **Exercise Forgiveness:**Forgiveness is an effective tool for developing self-love. It entails letting go of resentment, hatred, and bitterness toward oneself and others. We can release negative emotions and build a more positive and caring attitude toward ourselves by practicing forgiveness.

- **Exercise Self-Reflection:**Self-reflection is a practice that entails pausing to consider our ideas, emotions, and behaviors. It can assist us in identifying areas where we can improve and make adjustments in our lives. We can nurture self-love and acquire a deeper awareness of ourselves by practicing self-reflection.

To summarise, cultivating self-awareness, gratitude, self-compassion, self-care, setting boundaries, forgiveness, and self-reflection demands a purposeful effort. We can live a more satisfying and happier life if we practice these habits on a regular basis and create a strong sense of self-worth, self-acceptance, and self-confidence.

Chapter 9 Overcoming Obstacles to Self-Love

Despite the obvious advantages of self-love, there are numerous difficulties that can make it difficult to practice. Past traumas, bad self-talk, and feelings of unworthiness can all be hurdles. This chapter will offer helpful hints and tactics for overcoming these challenges and establishing a more loving relationship with yourself.

Self-love is an essential component of leading a happy and meaningful life. Accepting and embracing yourself for who you are, flaws and all, is what it implies. Unfortunately, many people struggle with self-love because of a variety of challenges that can be difficult to overcome. In this chapter, we will look at some of the most prevalent self-love roadblocks and offer practical solutions for overcoming them.

Negative self-talk is a major impediment to self-love. It's the voice in your head telling you that you're not good enough, clever enough, or attractive enough. It can be difficult to overcome negative self-talk, but it is necessary for your well-being.

Positive affirmations are one method for combating negative self-talk. Positive affirmations are phrases that you repeat to yourself to strengthen your positive attributes. "I am worthy of love and respect," "I am capable and strong," and "I am enough just as I am."

Mindfulness is another technique for combating negative self-talk. The practise of being present in the moment and noticing your thoughts without judgment is known as mindfulness. When you notice negative self-talk, acknowledge it and then let it go without lingering on it.

Comparison to others is a typical impediment to self-love. It's all too tempting to believe that everyone else is doing better than you. This way of thinking, however, is harmful to your self-esteem and well-being.

Focus on your own journey to escape the habit of comparing yourself to others. Remember that everyone follows their own path in life, and it's alright if yours differs from others. Set significant goals for yourself and work towards them at your own speed.

It is also beneficial to practice thankfulness. Take the time to appreciate what you have and the progress you've made toward your goals. You will feel more pleased and fulfilled if you focus on what you have rather than what you lack.

Perfectionism is an impediment to self-love since perfection is impossible. Setting unrealistic expectations for oneself sets you up for failure and disappointment.

Begin by creating more realistic expectations for yourself in order to overcome perfectionism. Recognize that making mistakes is a normal part of the learning process and that perfection is impossible to achieve.

Exercise self-compassion. Treat yourself with the same compassion and understanding that you would extend to a friend in need. Remember that you're doing your best, and that's all that matters.

Another impediment to self-love is fear of failure. You may avoid taking risks or trying new things if you are frightened of failing. This worry may prevent you from reaching your greatest potential.

Reframe your thinking to overcome your fear of failing. Instead of focusing on the negative consequences of failure, consider the good consequences of taking chances. Consider "What's the worst that can happen?" before moving on to the best-case scenario.

Exercise self-compassion. Keep in mind that making mistakes is a normal aspect of learning and growing. Treat yourself with compassion and understanding, and don't punish yourself if things don't go as planned.

To summarise, overcoming self-love hurdles can be a difficult but important task in order to live a happier and more rewarding life. Negative self-talk, comparison to others, perfectionism, and fear of failure are all barriers to developing self-love. However, by using positive affirmations, mindfulness, gratitude, realistic expectations, self-compassion, and reframing your thinking, you may overcome these obstacles and create a greater feeling of self-love. Remember that self-love is a journey that requires patience, kindness, and perseverance to complete. However, the benefits of self-love are well worth the effort because it leads to better self-acceptance, inner serenity, and a more fulfilling life.

Chapter 10 Forgiveness and Self-Love

Forgiveness is an essential component of self-love. When we keep grudges and resentments, we carry negative energy with us that can weigh us down and stifle our growth. In this chapter, we'll look at the relationship between self-love and forgiveness, as well as practical advice for practicing forgiveness towards yourself and others. We will also look at the function of self-forgiveness in fostering self-love.

Forgiveness and self-love are two intertwined concepts that are critical to our emotional well-being and overall pleasure. Forgiveness is the act of letting go of resentment, wrath, and other unpleasant feelings towards oneself or others for a previous transgression, mistake, or harm. In contrast, self-love is the practice of building a positive and supportive connection with oneself, which includes self-acceptance, self-respect, and self-care. In this chapter, we'll look at the connection between forgiveness and self-love, as well as the advantages of both and some practical methods for nurturing both.

The Relationship Between Self-Love and Forgiveness

Forgiveness and self-love are inextricably intertwined because they both include accepting ourselves and others as they are, flaws and all. Forgiveness is an act of self-kindness because it allows us to let go of bad emotions and move on with our lives. It also assists us in letting go of self-blame and self-criticism, both of which are harmful to our self-esteem and self-worth.

Self-love, on the other side, is the acceptance of oneself and the treatment of oneself with kindness, compassion, and respect. We may approach ourselves with more warmth and self-compassion when we forgive ourselves for our faults. As a result, a positive self-image and a healthy sense of self-worth are promoted.

Furthermore, when we forgive people for their faults, we make room for self-awareness and compassion. Forgiving others can assist us in releasing our anger and resentment, which can be a barrier to self-love. It enables us to see ourselves and others more positively, which is critical for developing good relationships and boosting emotional well-being.

The Advantages of Forgiveness and Self-Love

- Forgiveness and self-love are both necessary for our emotional health and happiness. The following are some of the advantages of practicing forgiveness and self-love:

- Stress and anxiety are reduced because forgiveness and self-love encourage pleasant emotions while decreasing negative ones such as wrath, resentment, and self-criticism. This can lead to less tension and worry.

- Improved mental health When we forgive ourselves and others, we release unpleasant feelings that can lead to despair, anxiety, and other mental health problems. Self-love fosters a positive self-image, which is also necessary for mental wellness. Connections that are healthier and more positive: Forgiveness and self-love assist us in developing healthier and more positive connections with ourselves and others. When we let go of our resentment and anger, we may approach others with more empathy and understanding, resulting in stronger bonds.

- Increased Resilience self-love and forgiveness promote emotional resilience, making it easier to recover from failures and hardships.

How to Develop Forgiveness and Self-Love

- **Self-Compassion:**When we make mistakes or feel negative emotions, we should treat ourselves with care and understanding. It entails accepting that we are human and fallible and that making mistakes is normal. Writing down our thoughts and feelings in a journal might help us process and release negative emotions. Writing about our forgiving and self-love experiences can also help us reflect on our progress and find areas for development.

- **Mindfulness:**Mindfulness practice can help us become more aware of our thoughts and feelings, allowing us to respond to them in a more positive and productive manner.

- **Seek Help:**Seeking help from friends, family, or a therapist can assist us in processing our feelings and working towards forgiveness and self-love.

Finally, forgiveness and self-love are two interconnected concepts that are critical for our mental and emotional well-being. Forgiveness practice assists us in releasing negative emotions, letting go of self-blame, and promoting a positive self-image. Self-love, on the other hand, entails treating oneself with kindness, compassion, and respect in order to foster a healthy feeling of self-worth. We may reduce stress and anxiety, enhance our mental health, develop healthier relationships, and boost our emotional resilience by practicing forgiveness and self-love. Self-compassion, journaling, mindfulness, and seeking help from others are all important ways to foster forgiveness and self-love. Overall, forgiveness and self-love are effective skills for leading better and more satisfying lives.

Chapter 11 Conclusion

Self-love is more than a slogan or a transient fad. It is a daring act that necessitates bravery, openness, and a willingness to face our deepest fears and insecurities. We may establish a more positive relationship with ourselves and improve all aspects of our life by prioritizing self-love.

Self-love is neither a transitory fad nor a trendy slogan. It is a daring act that necessitates bravery, openness, and a willingness to face our deepest fears and insecurities. We may establish a more positive relationship with ourselves and improve all aspects of our life by prioritizing self-love.

We've talked about what self-love is and isn't, as well as the roles of self-acceptance, vulnerability, and honesty in the process of building self-love. We've also looked at how self-love can be a strong weapon for overcoming self-doubt and self-criticism, as well as healing emotional wounds from our past.

Finally, we've included actionable steps for making self-love a daily habit, such as journaling, mindfulness, and affirmations. We hope that these tactics have given you the confidence to prioritize your own well-being and make self-love a habit rather than a one-time event.

Remember that self-love is not the same as selfishness. It is a courageous and bold act of self-care. We become better spouses, friends, and colleagues when we prioritize our own well-being. We have increased our productivity, resilience, and compassion for others.

So, keep prioritizing your own well-being and remember that self-love is a journey, not a destination. It will be difficult at times, but with practice and patience, you will be able to create a more loving and caring relationship with yourself.

Thank you for joining us on this path to self-love. We wish you continued success in your search for radical self-love.

9 789356 677142